The Library of Living and Working in Colonial Times™

A Day in the Life of a Colonial Silversmith

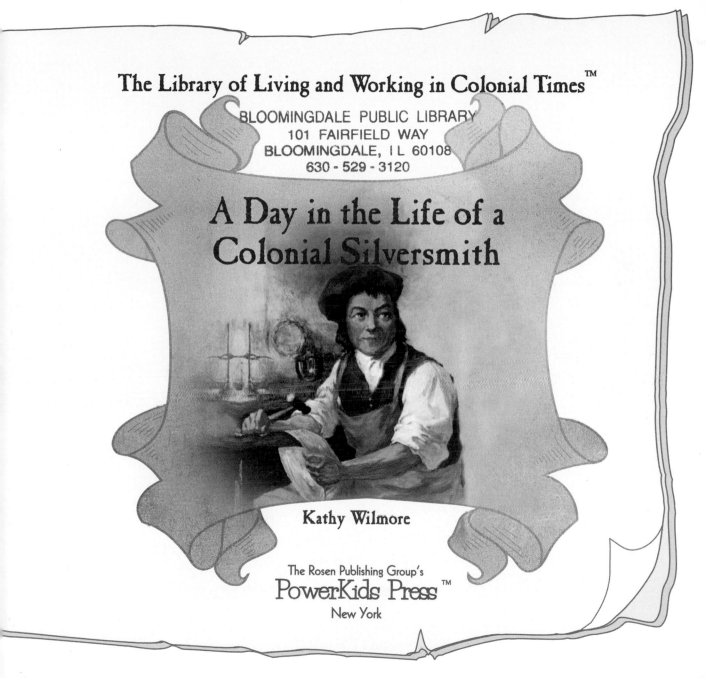

Kathy Wilmore

The Rosen Publishing Group's
PowerKids Press™
New York

To Bryan Brown, for the encouragement, humor, and grace that helped so much as I wrote this book—and to my mother, Julia C. Wilmore, who got me started.

Published in 2000 by The Rosen Publishing Group, Inc.
29 East 21st Street, New York, NY 10010

First Edition

Book design: Danielle Primiceri

Photo Credits: Cover and title pg © CORBIS-Bettmann; pp. 4, 7 © North Wind Picture Archives; pp. 8, 11, 15, 16, 20 © Archive Photos; p. 12 © The Granger Collection, New York; p. 19 © Joe Viesti/Viesti Associates, Inc.

Wilmore, Kathy.
  A day in the life of a Colonial silversmith / by Kathy Wilmore.
       p. cm. — (The Library of living and working in Colonial times)
Includes index.
Summary: Describes a day in the life of a Colonial silversmith, what he made and how he made it, and his dealings with his apprentices and customers.
  ISBN: 0-8239-5427-7 (lib. bdg. : alk. paper)
  1. Silverwork, Colonial—United States—Juvenile literature. [1. Silverwork. 2. United States—History—Colonial period, ca. 1600-1775.] I. Title. II. Series.
NK7112.W57 1999
739.2'3774'09033—dc21   99-11914
                                                                CIP
                                                                 AC

Manufactured in the United States of America

Lionel Curtis and his shop are fictional, but the details in this story about Colonial silversmiths and Colonial life are true.

Contents

Colonial America

In the early years of America's history, most things were made by hand. A silversmith was an important part of his community. Life in America was new and difficult for the British **colonists**, who had moved far from their homes. The work that skilled craftsmen like silversmiths did helped the **colonies** grow.

Colonial America was the period from about 1607 until 1776. That was before colonists in America declared their **independence** from Britain.

◀ *The first British colonists in New England came aboard the Mayflower.*

Not Just Jewelry

A smith is someone who makes objects by heating and hammering metal into a shape. Blacksmiths use iron, goldsmiths use gold, and silversmiths use silver and pewter. Pewter is an **alloy**, a mixture of several different metals.

A Colonial silversmith made jewelry, but he also made objects that people used in their homes every day. He made plates, trays, cups, bowls, spoons, knives, and forks. He made pitchers, salt shakers, candlesticks, buckles for belts and shoes, and even buttons and pins.

Silversmiths made many items that families used every day. ▶

Learning the Craft

Back in Britain, many families had always been farmers. Moving to America gave them the chance for a new life. A boy named Lionel Curtis could draw beautiful pictures and designs. A silversmith liked his drawings and agreed to take him as his **apprentice**.

Many Colonial boys began learning the silversmiths' trade at around age 14. Lionel Curtis served as an apprentice for seven years. Then he worked as the silversmith's **assistant** until he became a master at his craft.

◀ *This picture shows some of the many different ways that silversmiths did their work.*

A Shop of His Own

Many Colonial shoppers preferred the latest fashions in silver goods from England to those made in America. When Mr. Curtis opened his own shop, he often ordered jewelry, platters, and other items from England for people who preferred things made there. He and his assistants made many of the other objects sold in the shop. Sometimes **customers** asked Mr. Curtis to copy the latest patterns and designs from Europe and make them himself.

Large ships from Europe arrive in America carrying gold and silver goods and other items for colonists to buy. ▶

From Old to New

Colonial silversmiths often melted down old silver objects to make new ones. They also used silver coins. There were no banks, so turning silver into household items helped people protect it. It was easy to recognize if it got stolen. If they needed money, people could take their silver to be made into coins.

If a customer wanted a new set of plates and **tableware**, she gave the silversmith her old silver tableware and maybe some silver coins. The silversmith would melt down all this silver to make the new items.

◄ *Customers brought silversmiths their old tableware and picked out designs for their new set.*

Where the Action Was

A day in a silversmith's workshop, like Mr. Curtis's, usually began with his apprentice starting the fire in the **forge**. The forge was a huge fireplace that the silversmith used to melt silver and pewter. The apprentice used a **bellows** to pump air into the fire so that it would burn hotter. Many tools used for hammering, cutting, or twisting metal into shape hung from the walls. Workers sat at tables near windows using sunlight to help them see when they were making small objects, like pins or watch chains.

A large and very busy silversmith's shop. ▶

Heating and Hammering

Mr. Curtis melted down some of a customer's silver. After it cooled, he hammered it into sheets of the right thickness. Then he hammered, heated, and hammered the metal sheet until he had shaped it into a platter. Silver is a soft metal, so it is easy to shape this way. He did the same thing, again and again, for each plate and cup. For spoons and forks, Mr. Curtis melted the silver, then poured it into a specially designed **mold**. The silver cooled into the shape of that mold.

◀ *These workers are pressing and pounding metal into different shapes.*

A Work of Art

Once Mr. Curtis had shaped each plate, cup, or other item, one of his assistants polished it until it was shiny and smooth. Then Mr. Curtis went to work on the design. Sometimes a customer chose a pattern that she wanted for her new set of tableware. It might have had fancy curves and swirls or her family's initials on it. A silversmith had to cut or stamp this pattern into each item. He used special tools, including tiny hammers, to curve, press, and twist the metal into the designs.

This well-set table shows the results of a silversmith's hard work. ▶

Making His Mark

When Mr. Curtis finished his work, he stamped each item with his special mark. Some silversmiths had a style so **unique** that people could recognize their work without even looking at their marks!

The most famous Colonial silversmith, Paul Revere, is remembered for something other than his work at a forge. In 1775, Paul Revere made his famous "midnight ride" from Boston to the countryside. He rode to warn Americans that British troops were coming, just before the American Revolution began.

◀ *Paul Revere (1735-1818), America's most famous silversmith.*

A Bright Future

Colonial silversmiths worked quickly. An entire tableware set could be ready in one day! Customers often paid silversmiths with the silver leftover from the job. When customers were pleased with a silversmith's work, they often promised to send their friends to the silversmith's shop. Soon, most people stopped looking to England for their handmade goods and went to American silversmiths instead.

Web Sites:

http://www.history.org/life/trades/tradesil.htm
http://www.history.org/places/geddy/geddysil.htm

Glossary

alloy (AL-loy) A substance made by blending two or more pure metals.

apprentice (uh-PREN-tis) A young person learning a skill or trade.

assistant (uh-SIS-tent) Someone who helps another person.

bellows (BEL-ohz) A device that pumps air in and out; a blower.

colonist (KAH-luh-nist) A person who lives in a colony.

colony (KAH-luh-nee) A group of people who leave their own country to settle in another land but still remain under the rule of their old country.

customer (KUS-tuh-mer) A person who buys goods or services from someone else.

forge (FORJ) A furnace or shop with a furnace where metal is heated.

independence (in-dee-PEN-dents) Freedom from the control, support, influence, or help of others.

mold (MOLD) A hollow object used to give shape to what is put inside it.

tableware (TAY-bul-ware) The dishes, cups or glasses, and utensils (knives, forks, and spoons) used at a dinner table.

unique (yoo-NEEK) One-of-a-kind.

Index